Noven
Patron of Hopeless and Desperate Cases

"Naked I came forth from my mother's womb, and naked shall I go back there. The LORD gave and the LORD has taken away; blessed be the name of the LORD (Job 1:21)!"

"We accept good things from God; should we not accept evil (Job 2:10)?"

"By hearsay I had heard of you, but now my eye has seen you. Therefore I disown what I have said and repent in dust and ashes (Job 42:5-6)."

"Praise the LORD, for he is good; for his mercy endures forever; (Ps 136: 1)."

Novena to St. Jude
Patron of Hopeless and Desperate Cases

Nihil Obstat and Imprimatur received on
June 3, 2020
Archdiocese of Galveston-Houston, His
Eminence Daniel Cardinal DiNardo

Novena to St. Jude
Patron of Hopeless and Desperate Cases

A Short History of St. Jude

The apostle St. Jude is distinguished from Iscariot by the surname Thaddeus. Thaddeus means *praising or confessing* in Syriac. He is referred to as Lebbaeus which means *man with heart or courage.* This name indicates a man with understanding in Hebrew but comes from the word *Leb* which also means *heart* and can also signify *Lion*[i].

St. Jude was the brother of St. James the Less. Catholic belief is that Jude, the brother of Jesus and the author of the epistle of Jude are the same person. According to the surviving fragments of the work by Apostolic Father Papias of Hierapolis, *Exposition of the Sayings of the Lord,* Thaddeus is identified as the

3

son of Mary the wife of Cleophas, who was the mother of James the bishop and apostle, of Simeon, Joseph and Thaddeus. Hence by referring to Jude as the "brother" of Jesus, Jude is a maternal cousin of the Lord as is James who was the martyred bishop of Jerusalem[ii].

More praiseworthy than St. Jude's blood relation to Our Lord was his contempt for the world, and his zeal, love and suffering for the sake of the Gospel. Nothing is said about St. Jude in the Gospels before his name is listed with that of the other apostles. After spending much time in prayer, Jesus decided to choose 12 men, 12 unlikely candidates, who would be his apostles and proclaim the Kingdom of God to all people. Simon the Zealot was one of those 12 who were called. The Zealots were a

Novena to St. Jude
Patron of Hopeless and Desperate Cases

Jewish group who believed that the Messiah would herald a free and independent Jewish nation. At that time Judea was occupied by Rome and had to pay tribute to Cesar. Some Zealots also were concerned that the spiritual ideals of Judaism be observed. Others in the group acted more like modern-day terrorists, raiding, killing, and inciting riots. Simon was referred to as "the zealot" to distinguish him from Simon Peter as well.

At the same time St. Jude was called, he was most likely a fisherman by trade. Along with 10 other men, Jude and Simon, followed Jesus, lived with him, fled when he underwent his Passion, and rejoiced when he rose from the dead. At the last supper, Our Lord promised to manifest Himself to everyone that would

Novena to St. Jude
Patron of Hopeless and Desperate Cases

love Him. St. Jude asked if the Lord meant manifesting to the apostles or the world. This indicates the expectation of a secular kingdom. The response given by the Lord indicates a more personal and spiritual kingdom of love beginning within the interior life of those that love God (Jn 14:22-24).

After the Lord's ascension and the descent of the Holy Spirit, St. Jude and the other apostles went forth armed with the Holy Spirit and the name of Jesus to preach the Good News. They also healed the sick, gave sight to the blind and overcame the powers of darkness with the light of truth. One tradition is that Thaddeus was sent to Edessa to aid King Agbar who was suffering from leprosy. According to the legend, King Agbar

Novena to St. Jude
Patron of Hopeless and Desperate Cases

was cured of leprosy upon seeing the image of the Lord's face that St. Jude brought with him. Allegedly Agbar hoped to have the Lord himself come to heal him. St. Jude was sent instead due to the demands of the Lord's ministry and His focus on the children of Israel.

It is believed that St. Jude preached up and down Judea, Samaria, Syria and particularly Mesopotamia. He returned to Jerusalem in the year 62 C.E. after the martyrdom of his brother, James the Less. His brother had been bishop there until thrown to his death from the temple by Jews. St. Jude also traveled to what is modern day Iraq and Iran. There is also some belief that St. Jude brought the Gospel to Armenia as well. At Pentecost

Novena to St. Jude
Patron of Hopeless and Desperate Cases

both Jude and Simon were filled with the Spirit and a burning desire to spread the Good News. Jude traveled to Mesopotamia to preach while Simon went to Egypt. Eventually they both ended up in Persia, modern-day Iran. There they worked together evangelizing people until they were both martyred. St. Jude is portrayed in art with a club since it is commonly believed that he was clubbed to death. Simon appears with a saw due to the understanding he was severed into pieces. These two apostles witnessed to the risen Lord with their lives. After his death, the body of Saint Jude was brought from Beirut to Rome and was placed in a crypt in the great basilica of Saint Peter. Today, the church commemorates his death on the

Novena to St. Jude
Patron of Hopeless and Desperate Cases

28th of October, along with his companion St. Simon the apostle. St. Jude is invoked by people in times of hopelessness and is referred to as the patron of hopeless cases[iii].

We do owe God eternal praise and thanks for the infinite mercy by which he established His church on earth and sends us His sanctifying grace. The same Spirit that was present at Pentecost now descends on the Church built upon the foundation laid by St. Jude and the other apostles. The Lord came to liberate us from sin and the spirit of the world. We can either come to love and choose Him, or the world and ourselves. St. Jude preached the promise of restored unity between God and man through the sacrifice of Christ. In the sermon on the mount our Lord said, "seek first the kingdom [of God] and his righteousness, and all these things will be given you besides (Mt 6:33)." Go to God through St. Jude. The world only holds empty promises and half-truths. "He has set before you fire and water to whichever you choose, stretch forth your hand. Before man are life and death, good and evil, whichever he chooses shall be given him (Sir 15:15-16)."

Novena to St. Jude
Patron of Hopeless and Desperate Cases

Prayer Said Every Day of Novena

St. Jude apostle, martyr and true relative of Jesus, Mary, and Joseph. I come to you with faith and trust in your intercession before the throne of God. I praise the Holy One for Himself and His Spirit that emanates from Him, throughout all of heaven, and throughout all of creation. Through your prayers may the Spirit of God come upon me with the same power that gave you the courage to be His witness and bring the gospel to others. Humbly before you I ask you to pray with me to the Lord for the grace of _____. I am grateful for your assistance and thank you for now until I might there remain to praise and thank God for ever. Amen. God's will be done. St. Jude please pray for us.

Novena to St. Jude
Patron of Hopeless and Desperate Cases

Day One; Faith and Truthfulness.

Faith: "For if you do not believe that I AM, you will die in your sins (Jn 8:24)."

Truthfulness: "He willed to give us birth by the word of truth that we may be a kind of firstfruits of his creatures (Jas 1:18)."

St. Jude, as an apostle filled with the holy spirit at Pentecost, you boldly proclaimed the truth about God every day until your martyrdom. You were eyewitness to the fact that Jesus had power over nature, sickness, deformities, demons and even death. You were commissioned to go forth and baptize all in the name of the Father, Son and Holy Spirt, and teach what had been

Novena to St. Jude
Patron of Hopeless and Desperate Cases

commanded you as you witnessed His ascension. By the power of His name and the Holy Spirit you healed the lame and ill, cast out demons and preformed other miracles to make salvation known. As part of the foundation of God's church, you had an urgency to make the good news of salvation known. No man could pay the price of his own salvation, nor that of others. God Himself, in the person of Yeshua, came to pay a debt we owe because we cannot. Thanks be to the eternal Father that his Son came to save what had been lost and reconcile all things into Himself. St. Jude please pray for me that I may increase in faith, hope, and love as I see to imitate Christ. Amen.

Novena to St. Jude
Patron of Hopeless and Desperate Cases

1x Our Father, Hail Mary, St. Jude apostle, martyr and true relative of Jesus and Mary pray for us, Glory be.

Day Two; Hope and Confidence.

Hope: "For I know well the plans I have in mind for you-oracle of the LORD-plans for your welfare and not for woe, so as to give you a future of hope (Jer 29:11)."

Confidence: "But you will receive power when the holy Spirit comes upon you, and you will be my witnesses in Jerusalem, throughout Judea and Samaria, and to the ends of the earth (Acts 1:8)."

St. Jude, you were present with the mother of Our Lord and the other

Novena to St. Jude
Patron of Hopeless and Desperate Cases

apostles at Pentecost and received the
outpouring of the holy spirit. This was
promised by the Lord and is how He set
the world on fire. You and the others
had been hiding behind locked doors
since the crucifixion. Now, baptized in
the Spirit, the apostles all poured out
into the streets boldly proclaiming the
truth of Jesus Christ. You were heard in
languages that neither you, nor the other
apostles knew. All those traveling from
afar heard the message of salvation
being spoken in their own language. So
marvelous was this witness that 3000
converted that day as the church was
established. Empowered by the Spirit of
God, you began your ministry and made
the good news known. Your mission
was now to touch as many lives as

15

Novena to St. Jude
Patron of Hopeless and Desperate Cases

possible in the name of Jesus. So bold
and persistent were your efforts that you
were killed by those who preferred the
darkness. You and Simon were killed
by those that would not or could not see
the light. I can imagine that your final
words may have included a request for
God to have mercy on your attackers. St.
Jude, please pray for me that I, too, may
have the confidence of true faith and
firm hope that will allow me to live the
gospel, forgive those that harm me, and
happily make sacrifices for my
neighbors and enemies. Amen.

*1x Our Father, Hail Mary, St. Jude
apostle, martyr and true relative of
Jesus and Mary pray for us, Glory be*

Novena to St. Jude
Patron of Hopeless and Desperate Cases

Day Three; Agape and Philia Love.

Love/Agape: The unconditional love of God for man and love of man for God. "For I am convinced that neither death, nor life, nor angels, nor principalities, nor present things, nor future things, nor powers, nor height, nor depth, nor any other creature will be able to separate us from the love of God in Christ Jesus our Lord (Rm 8:38-39)."

Love/Philia: "Compassion and brotherly love: "I give you a new commandment: love one another. As I have loved you, so you also should love one another (Jn 8:34)."

St. Jude you were a "brother" by blood of the Lord and a close companion

17

during his ministry. You proved that
"love is strong as death (Sg 8:6)" by
dying a martyr's death. You proclaimed
the gospel out of love for others that
they might be saved. Laboring in the
Father's vineyard, you sought to sew as
many seeds as possible to yield an
abundant harvest. Christ came first to
the Jews but commissioned you and the
other apostles to go the ends of the earth
proclaiming the truth of His saving love.
The Talmud states, if one saves another
person, they save the world. There is no
specification as to what that person
looks like, where they come from, how
much or little they have, or any other
specific "need" that makes one worthy
to be saved. The good news is that if
Adam only had one son, the Son of God

would have willingly come to relieve the curse the world was under. In His deeply personal love that he has with each of us, He did come suffer, die, and was resurrected as if we are the only person in existence. He bore the cross for each of us and each one of us is the very apple of His eye. His love of you is infinite, limitless, and unconditional. St. Jude please pray that I may appreciate the tremendous love of God and realize it is river that must flow in and through me to others. Water that does not flow becomes stagnant and is good for nothing. May I also have the type of love that gives even in pain imitating the Lord and you in your sacrifice for enemies and those that do not know Him. Amen.

Novena to St. Jude
Patron of Hopeless and Desperate Cases

1x Our Father, Hail Mary, St. Jude apostle, martyr and true relative of Jesus and Mary pray for us, Glory be.

Day Four; Fortitude and Perseverance.

Fortitude: "The signs of an apostle were performed among you with all endurance, signs and wonders, and mighty deeds (2 Cor 12:12)."

Perseverance: "Then he said to all, 'If anyone wishes to come after me, he must deny himself and take up his cross daily and follow me (Lk 9:23)…the one who perseveres to the end will be saved (Mt 24:13)."

St. Jude, you persevered to the end and gave your life in the service of Our Lord.

Novena to St. Jude
Patron of Hopeless and Desperate Cases

You had direct knowledge of Our Lord who knowing the cross was eminent, worked tirelessly to personally touch, heal, help, and preach the truth about Himself. He revealed the Father, the nature of the world, life and what awaits those who obey Him.

There is mention in the gospels of Our Lord fasting (Mt 4:2), losing sleep to pray in isolation (Mt 14:23) and walking to the extent he all but collapsed upon arriving at a destination (Jn 4:6). Crowds would press upon Our Lord as he came and went from town to town on foot. He addressed large crowds and engaged individuals intensely and passionately

21

giving of himself daily until His "heart became like wax; it melts within me (Ps 22:15)." After life had left His body, blood and water gushed forth from his chest as further oblation. St. Teresa of Calcutta said that it must hurt, at least a little bit, if one is truly giving oneself in love. The Lord gave to the point of saying "My God, My God why have you abandoned me (Ps 22:2)?"

St. Jude, I may not be called to be a martyr as you were. If I am, may the Lord give me the grace to do so with courage. Please also pray with me for the grace to prefer death over purposefully offending Him, and to appreciate serving others over being served. Amen.

1x Our Father, Hail Mary, St. Jude apostle, martyr and true relative of Jesus and Mary pray for us, Glory be.

Day Five; Justice and Equity:

Justice: "Make justice your aim: redress the wronged, hear the orphan's plea, defend the widow. Come now, let us set things right, says the LORD (Is 1:17-18)."

Equity: "You have a mighty arm. Your hand is strong; your right hand is ever exalted. Justice and judgment are the

Novena to St. Jude
Patron of Hopeless and Desperate Cases

foundation of your throne; mercy and faithfulness march before you (Ps 89:14-15)."

St. Jude, you were baptized with the Holy Spirit in the upper room at Pentecost. During Our Lord's earthly ministry, he sent forth disciples ahead of him to announce His coming and empowered them to heal, help and cast out demons in His name. St. Jude you continued this work of God's justice and making His real presence known in the eucharist. You also made known His kingdom by reclaiming what had been lost in the fall. Biblical justice entails mercy and making right what has been broken in nature,

Novena to St. Jude
Patron of Hopeless and Desperate Cases

human nature, the world, and the
universe. Jesus announced his public
ministry by stating; "The spirit of the
Lord GOD is upon me, because the
LORD has anointed me; He has sent me
to bring good news to the afflicted, to
bind up the brokenhearted, To proclaim
liberty to the captives, release to the
prisoners, To announce a year of favor
from the LORD and a day of vindication
by our God; To comfort all who mourn;
(Is 61:1-3)." When one speaks of
"Justice" in western society frequently
what is intended is "condemnation" or
"vengeance." The Lord made it clear he
was bringing empathy, love and
compassion as His miracles reversed,

Novena to St. Jude
Patron of Hopeless and Desperate Cases

sickness, deformity, evil, and death. St.
Jude you imitated this and continued by
invoking the Holy Spirit and the name of
Jesus to make manifest this same love
and compassion of God through healings,
signs and casting out evil. St. Paul states,
"Therefore, just as through one person
sin entered the world, and through sin,
death, and thus death came to all,
inasmuch as all sinned (Rm 5:12)...
(and) For if by that one person's
transgression the many died, how much
more did the grace of God and the
gracious gift of the one person Jesus
Christ overflow for the many (Rm 5:15)."
St. Jude please pray for me that I may be

merciful to others since He has been so gracious and merciful to me. Amen.

1x Our Father, Hail Mary, St. Jude apostle, martyr and true relative of Jesus and Mary pray for us, Glory be.

Day Six; Wisdom and Prudence.

Wisdom: "But the wisdom from above is first of all pure, then peaceable, gentle, compliant, full of mercy and good fruits, without inconstancy or insincerity (Jas 3:17)."

Prudence: "I, Wisdom, dwell with prudence, and useful knowledge I have (Prv 8:12)." "The astute see an evil and hide, while the naive continue on and pay the penalty (Prv 22:3)."

St. Jude, Our Lord said to be "wise as serpents and simple as doves (Mt 10:16)." You and the other 11 disciples were sent forth with the authority to drive out unclean spirits and heal in His name. Here you were "one sent" to proclaim the good news of the Lord and His presence among us. Then, as now, the world was full of sin and hostile to Truth and the Truth of God. "And this is the verdict, that the light came into the world, but people preferred darkness to light, because their works were evil (Jn 3:19)." The darkness sought to

Novena to St. Jude
Patron of Hopeless and Desperate Cases

overcome Our Lord in His crucifixion,
but that made the glory of His
resurrection a more blinding light. St.
Jude, help me to always be aware that no
matter how black the darkness, it is
powerless to put out the smallest candle.
May the spark of the Holy Spirit within
me sing that I am a child of the Eternal
Father. May the knowledge of this
essential truth be the light that guides me
in navigating life. May I choose good
over evil, avoid sin, and come to a real
relationship with Our Lord. May I come
to know God as He truly is and not as I
would have Him be. St. Jude, please pray
with me that I may be able to return some
of the Love that has been given to me by

Novena to St. Jude
Patron of Hopeless and Desperate Cases

my Maker. He has given me an entire universe that screams of His magnificence, beauty, and power. May I be centered in the knowledge of His love for me though I may be limited in my understanding. St. Jude please help me strive to know Him and all things pertaining to Him. He is the pearl of great prize and these are the only things worth knowing. The only way through life to eternal life are choices that lead to Him.

1x Our Father, Hail Mary, St. Jude apostle, martyr and true relative of Jesus and Mary pray for us, Glory be.

Novena to St. Jude
Patron of Hopeless and Desperate Cases

Day Seven; Temperance and Self-Denial.

Temperance: "From within people, from their hearts, come evil thoughts, unchastity, theft, murder, adultery, greed, malice, deceit, licentiousness, envy, blasphemy, arrogance, folly. All these evils come from within and they defile (Mk 7:21-23)."

Self-Denial: "Beloved, I urge you as aliens and sojourners to keep away from worldly desires that wage war against the soul (1 Pt 2:11)."

St. Jude, you heard the Lord say: "Can the wedding guests mourn as long as the bridegroom is with them? The days will come when the bridegroom is taken away from them, and then they will fast (Mt 9:15)." Another time you heard him say "I have food to eat of which you do not know (Jn 4:32)." Help me to understand that all things that God has made are good and meant for their appropriate use and purpose. Ask Our Lord to grant that I may have the wisdom and help of His grace to exert self-control in areas where I am tempted. May I starve my lusts for food, pleasure, worldly excitement, power and prestige and other things that eclipse God as Lord of my life. St. Jude pray that I may have the willingness to mortify myself and avoid people, places

and things that are occasions of sin. It is
recorded that Our Lord only fasted once
in the desert when the enemy sought to
tempt Him. This allowed Him to be
closer to the Father and respond, "It is
not by bread alone that people live, but
by all that comes forth from the mouth of
the LORD (Dt 8:3)." The Holy Spirit
tells us, "Is this not, rather, the fast that I
choose: releasing those bound unjustly,
untying the thongs of the yoke; Setting
free the oppressed, breaking off every
yoke? Is it not sharing your bread with
the hungry, bringing the afflicted and the
homeless into your house; Clothing the
naked when you see them, and not
turning your back on your own flesh?

33

Novena to St. Jude
Patron of Hopeless and Desperate Cases

Then your light shall break forth like the dawn (Is 58: 6-8)." St. Jude, please pray for me that I may have the prudence not only to avoid evil but to do good.

1x Our Father, Hail Mary, St. Jude apostle, martyr and true relative of Jesus and Mary pray for us, Glory be.

Day Eight; Benevolence and Compassion.

Benevolence: "So then, while we have the opportunity, let us do good to all, but especially to those who belong to the family of the faith (Gal 3:10)."

Novena to St. Jude
Patron of Hopeless and Desperate Cases

Compassion: "Put on then, as God's chosen ones, holy and beloved, heartfelt compassion, kindness, humility, gentleness, and patience, bearing with one another and forgiving one another, if one has a grievance against another; as the Lord has forgiven you, so must you also do (Col 3:12-13)."

St. Jude, when you walked with Our Lord you saw how he was moved with compassion by those who were poor, hungry, lost, and in mental, emotional, and physical pain. You witnessed how He would personally come down to see the people at their eye level. He was not condescending to others though His very presence on earth was a great condescension. He could see each person as if they were the only soul in existence while surrounded by a crowd. It was true of the woman at the well, the woman taken in adultery, the man possessed by "Legion" and the one leper of ten who returned to thank Him. Our Lord knew when a single woman out of an entire crowd touched the hem of his garment and was moved with compassion. He saw the crowds that followed Him and said, "they are like sheep without a shepherd (Mk 6:34)." Seeing the Lord do such work and hear his words could only inspire one to follow Him. As "one sent" by the Lord you had the power of His

Novena to St. Jude
Patron of Hopeless and Desperate Cases

name to touch people the same way. St. Jude I can imagine you preaching the Good News of the Lord, laying hands on people, listening to concerns and thanking God for working His miracles through your prayers. St. Jude please pray that I, too, may be able to listen and respond to those in my life with humble compassion and empathy. That I may know that it is God in me who is touching others and not take credit for His work. Amen.

1x Our Father, Hail Mary, St. Jude apostle, martyr and true relative of Jesus and Mary pray for us, Glory be.

Novena to St. Jude
Patron of Hopeless and Desperate Cases

Day Nine; Courage and Valor:

Courage: "For God did not give us a spirit of cowardice but rather of power and love and self-control (2 Tim 1:7)."

Valor: "The way we came to know love was that he laid down his life for us; so, we ought to lay down our lives for our brothers (1 Jn 3:16)." "No one has greater love than this, to lay down one's life for one's friends. You are my friends if you do what I command you (Jn 15:13-14)."

St. Jude, it is written that you and the others fled at the Garden of Gethsemane and would meet in locked rooms in fear

Novena to St. Jude
Patron of Hopeless and Desperate Cases

until Pentecost. The power of God came to rest upon you, the other apostles, and the blessed mother in the upper room. Our Lord had instructed that the Holy Spirit would speak through you when "you are led away or handed over (Mk 13:11)" and give you power to be His witnesses "in Jerusalem, throughout Judea, in Samaria and to the ends of the earth (Acts 1:8)." Thus, armed with the Holy Name of Jesus and empowered by the Holy Spirit you were ready to boldly do battle with the world, sin, and the enemy. There is nothing in creation that could have kept you from proclaiming the truth of God in Christ Jesus. In His name and by the power of the cross you

Novena to St. Jude
Patron of Hopeless and Desperate Cases

converted people and established
churches. You and St. Simon were
traveling and evangelizing together in
Mesopotamia when you both were
martyred in your service to the Lord. He
was and is the Truth and Light and you
both were bringing that Light to others
who "preferred the darkness (Jn 3:19)."
Cut off from the Lord I can do (Jn 5:15)"
and be nothing. Please pray with me that,
like you, I may remain in and with the
Lord in my daily life and thereby be part
of His solution. May I have the grace of
preferring death over offending Our Lord
and the willingness to remain faithful to
Him. "For in him were created all things
in heaven and on earth, the visible and

Novena to St. Jude
Patron of Hopeless and Desperate Cases

the invisible, whether thrones or
dominions or principalities or powers; all
things were created through him and for
him (Col 1:16)." As a child of the Father
I was also made by and for the Lord
Jesus. Abiding in Him is the only thing
that can complete me. I realize
imperfectly now and will only understand
completely in His presence. There I hope
to remain to praise and thank Him for
ever. St. Jude please pray that I may be
united with God as his friend on earth
and forever in His heavenly kingdom.
Amen.

Novena to St. Jude
Patron of Hopeless and Desperate Cases

1x Our Father, Hail Mary, St. Jude apostle, martyr and true relative of Jesus and Mary pray for us, Glory be.

A Sperate Daily Prayer to St. Jude

St. Jude, apostle and true relative of Jesus, Mary, and Joseph,

I salute you through the Most Sacred Heart of Jesus.

Through this heart I praise and thank God for Himself and for the graces and privileges he has bestowed upon you.

To you has been assigned the privilege of aiding mankind in the most desperate cases.

Novena to St. Jude
Patron of Hopeless and Desperate Cases

Please come to my aid that I may praise the mercies of God.

I will be grateful to God and to you all the days of my life and be a faithful client until, as I hope, I may there remain to praise and thank God forever. May the Sacred Heart of Jesus be adored, worshiped, loved, and thanked in all the tabernacles of the world until the end of time, and forever in his kingdom of joy, happiness, and love. In the Glory of the Eternal Father and the unity of the Holy Spirit, One God forever and ever. Amen. 3x Glory be.

Novena to St. Jude
Patron of Hopeless and Desperate Cases

A Prayer for Spiritual Help

O Holy Apostle, Martyr and servant of Jesus Christ, St. Jude Thaddeus, you did spread the True Faith among the most barbarous and distant nations and did win the obedience of Jesus Christ many tribes of peoples by the power of His Holy Word.

Grant, I beg you, that from this day I may renounce every sinful habit, that I may be preserved from all evil thoughts, that I may always obtain your assistance, particularly in danger and difficulty, and that I may reach the heavenly country, with you to adore the Most Holy Trinity, God Our Father, His Son Jesus Christ Our Lord and Holy Ghost, forever and ever. Amen.

Novena to St. Jude
Patron of Hopeless and Desperate Cases

May the sacred heart of Jesus be adored, glorified, loved, and preserved throughout the world, now and forever. Amen.

A Prayer of Thanksgiving for Answered Needs

Most sweet Lord Jesus Christ, in union with the unutterable praises which the Holy Trinity extolls upon itself; which flow upon your holy and good mother, my guardian angel and all the angels and saints; I praise, glorify, bless and thank You most of all for the graces and privileges you have bestowed upon your good friend and chosen apostle St. Jude. Through his intercession, please come to my aid in all my needs and for the sake of his merits please deign to strengthen and protect me from my enemies. Amen. 3x Our Father, Hail Mary and Glory Be.

Novena to St. Jude
Patron of Hopeless and Desperate Cases

A Chaplet of St Jude

Said on chaplet consisting of three sets of three beads, With a medal at one end and a cross or crucifix on the other.

On the cross, say the following prayer: St. Jude, apostle, martyr and true relative of Jesus, Mary and Joseph, I salute you through the most sacred heart of Jesus; Through this heart I praise glorify and bless God most of all for Himself and for the graces and privileges He has bestowed upon you; Humbly here before you, I ask you to look down upon me and we who invoke you with compassion, Please despise not my petition and let not my trust be in vain. To you has been assigned the privilege

Novena to St. Jude
Patron of Hopeless and Desperate Cases

of aiding mankind in the most desperate cases, please come to my aid so that I may praise the mercies of God. I will be grateful to you all he days of my life until, as I hope, I may one day there remain to praise and thank God in a world without end. Amen.

On each of the 9 beads, pray the following:

One Hail Mary and the following invocation:

Saint Jude, Apostle martyr and relative of Our Lord Jesus Christ, Mary and Joseph, pray we who invoke you, those recommended to you, the church and the world.

Novena to St. Jude
Patron of Hopeless and Desperate Cases

At the end of the Chaplet, say the
following prayers:

May the Most Sacred Heart of Jesus be
adored and loved in all the tabernacles
until the end of time. Amen.

May the most Sacred Heart of Jesus be
praised and glorified now and forever.
Amen.
Saint Jude pray for us and hear our
prayers. Amen.

Blessed be the Sacred Heart of Jesus.
Blessed be the Immaculate Heart of
Mary.

Blessed be Saint Jude Thaddaeus
in all the world and for all Eternity.

Novena to St. Jude
Patron of Hopeless and Desperate Cases

(If one would like to say a forty-bead chaplet, the above Hail Mary and St. Jude invocations are repeated 40 times.)

**Novena to St. Jude
Patron of Hopeless and Desperate Cases**

Foot Notes

_____

[i] M.G. Easton M.A., D.D., Illustrated Bible Dictionary, Third Edition, published by Thomas Nelson, 1897

[ii] Papias of Hierapolis (lived c. 70–163 AD.) *Exposition of the Oracles of the Lord. Fragment X. earlychristianwritings.com.* Retrieved on 11/28/2019.

[iii] St Jude, (1999-2018). https://www.ecatholic2000.com/butler/vol10 /october102.shtml. Retrieved on 12/21/2019.

Printed in Great Britain
by Amazon